Make Spectacular Books

Fabulous Fabric, Skewer & Folded Books

C&T PUBLISHING

Sue Astroth

Text © 2006 Sue Astroth

Artwork © 2006 C&T Publishing, Inc.

Publisher: Amy Marson

Editorial Director: Gailen Runge

Acquisitions Editor: Jan Grigsby

Editor: Stacy Chamness

Copyeditor/Proofreader: Wordfirm Inc.

Cover Designer: Kristen Yenche

Design Director: Kristen Yenche

Illustrator: Tim Manibusan

Production Assistants: Zinnia Heinzmann and Kerry Graham

Photography: C&T Publishing, Inc., unless otherwise noted

Published by C&T Publishing, Inc., P.O. Box 1456, Lafayette, CA 94549

Library of Congress Cataloging-in-Publication Data

Astroth, Sue

  Make spectacular books : fabulous fabric, skewer & folded books / Sue Astroth.

    p. cm.

  ISBN-13: 978-1-57120-356-4 (paper trade)

  ISBN-10: 1-57120-356-7 (paper trade)

  1. Book design--Handbooks, manuals, etc. 2. Books--Handbooks, manuals, etc. 3. Textile fabrics. I. Title.

  TT896.3.A88 2006

  686--dc22

                                    2005031205

Printed in Singapore

10 9 8 7 6 5 4 3 2 1

Dedication

Mom, you taught me to appreciate the joy and wonder of books. They have taken me places I never dreamed of.

Acknowledgments

Thank you to my wonderful, loving friends who provide encouragement and support on a daily basis—Terrece S., Krista H., Vanessa O., Linda L., Olaitan V.C.S., and Phyllis N. Thank you all!

I also thank

- Barbara D. for showing me how to make my first skewer book.

- Elaine B. for always being there with a tip, suggestion, or loan of supplies.

- Scott, Josie, Melanie, and Megan for sharing your beautiful vacation photos and your memories of your trip for the *Sedona Memory* book. You guys are the best!

- My patient family for putting up with fabric, thread, and projects everywhere, endless questions about whether the project looks all right, late dinners, and a minor (?) mood swing or two!

- Jois—I couldn't do this without you—still!

- Sandy M. from Hoffman for the *Sedona Memory* book fabric.

- Emily Cohen for providing so many beautiful Timeless Treasures batik and novelty fabrics.

- Kathy and Tasha at Michael Miller Fabrics for beautiful fabric and fun fabric paper.

Contents

Introduction

I have been in love with books since I was a young child. When I was a kid, the library was one of my favorite places to go on a Saturday. The time I spent hanging out in the aisles and selecting what I wanted to read was magical. From the pages of a book I could go somewhere, learn a new craft, solve a mystery, or even attempt to do my homework. I still surround myself with books; there are stacks of them in every room of my house. Who knew that all these years later I would write a book about making books?

It all started as I was avoiding a deadline. I needed just a couple more projects for the book *Spectacular Cards*, but I didn't have a specific direction. I entered my studio unsure of where my creative muse would take me, so I started to clean. Although some in my family call cleaning a form of procrastination, I usually get a burst of creative inspiration while cleaning. Over in the corner was a big stack of prepared fabric I had been using as bases for fabric cards, and I began cutting them into more manageable pieces. I folded them into card sizes and stacked them up. My prepared fabric stack was starting to look a lot like a book I had recently made. Hmmm…why not make up books of various styles, using the prepared fabric pieces as covers? That thought was the beginning, and I'm still trying out new styles and patterns.

I hope you enjoy all the various book instructions I have prepared for you. I have included a few basic patterns as well as many more ideas on how to combine the patterns with your own fabric selections to create one-of-a-kind books to give as gifts, or to make as a special treat just for you.

Let's get started!

The Supplies

One

You really don't need a lot of tools to make the projects included in this book.

This chapter describes the products and tools I like to have handy while I am

working. Most of these supplies are readily available at your favorite sewing,

craft, or scrapbooking store. You probably even have some of them in your craft

room already.

❈ Fabric

A good-quality, 100 percent cotton is my fabric of choice for all my sewing and crafting projects. Most of my fabric books become scrapbooks, so I try to choose fabric that will give a hint about the story my scrapbook will tell. I can usually find a fabric to match just about any story.

I look for fabric everywhere—my local quilt shop, craft stores, garage sales, online auctions, and my friends' stashes. I have even been known to search the clothing section of thrift shops looking for fun and unusual fabrics to make into books.

Because the finished projects won't be washed, I do not usually prewash fabrics I buy at my trusted fabric store. I do break this rule, however, when I purchase a fabric from somewhere else.

I am often asked, "Exactly how much fabric should I buy?" For a basic book, I buy ½ yard of fabric or one fat quarter each of two complementary fabrics. That amount allows me to make one 6½-inch-square skewer book, leaving me with a few scraps for some extras, such as a small card, a matchbook, or a couple of tags. Ideally, I select a print for the outside of the cover and a companion print or solid for the inside of the cover; buying fat quarters allows me this option.

I once had a problem with a black print fabric from a discount store. The thread count wasn't very high, so the white base paper of my fabric book cloth showed through, leaving me with a less-than-desired finished look. Not all fabric from discount stores will create this type of problem; I have used many different fabrics successfully. Just remember to buy good quality, buy what you like, and take a minute to make a plan.

Most of the time, I tend to select fabrics with a directional print, but I don't always realize this until I'm ready to cut out my book. Although this isn't a bad thing, you should consider a couple of things about directional fabrics before you make a book.

- Will your selected book pattern show off your fabric design, or will part of the design end up upside down or backward?

- Are the prints on both the front and back covers going in the correct direction?

- You may need to purchase some extra fabric to ensure that you get the part of the design you want on both covers.

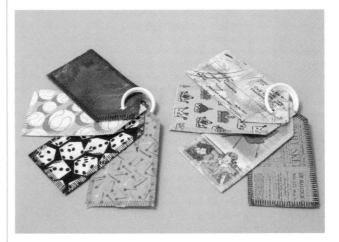

Nondirectional and directional prints

So far, most of my books have been made with cotton, but every now and then I try to break out of the box…just a little. I decided to try some scraps I had in the studio of a few fabric types just to see what kind of results I would get. I tried a Guatemalan fabric, some silk dupioni, and some unbleached linen. Each fabric produced a beautiful and interesting book, if I do say so myself. The only real change you need to make when you work with various fabrics is to make sure to match the heat setting on your iron to each fabric when fusing it to the fabric adhesive.

✖ Paper

BASE PAPER

Use a 24″ × 36″ sheet of 80-pound vellum-finish paper for the base of the prepared fabric book cloth. This size allows flexibility to make either large or small books, is readily available from paper stores, and most importantly, just happens to handle most fat quarters. Should you need a larger paper or prepared fabric, simply use paper adhesive to glue sheets together with a ¼–½″ overlap before fusing fabric to them.

It's always good to have a backup plan, though. I ran out of the base paper once and found I could use 12″ × 18″ drawing paper. This paper is available in pads at office-supply stores, drugstores, and discount stores, and it works almost as well.

BOOK PAGES

Start to think about what kind of paper you want to use for the pages of your book. Cardstock comes in such a wide variety of colors that I can almost always find one to match my chosen fabric. When I can't find just the right color match, I make my pages from white, cream, or black cardstock. All the cardstock I use for my books is acid free. One of my favorite fabric book sizes is 6½″ × 6½″. It's small, easy, and quick to finish, and it makes a great gift—and you can simply cut a 12″ × 12″ sheet of cardstock in half for the pages. Just one cut, and there isn't any waste! Another paper size to consider for the pages is 8½″ × 11″. Sometimes this size will be perfect for your book and might even eliminate some leftover scraps.

Making 6½″-square books allows me to use 12″ × 12″ cardstock, minimizing the possibility of cardstock scraps.

When book pages will be larger than 6″ × 12″, I use art paper, which can be found at craft and art stores. Available in a limited color selection, this paper is usually sold in 19″ × 25″ sheets. Because of their size, these sheets are great for making accordion inserts for your fabric books and covers. There are two styles of art paper: smooth, which is good for writing on, and textured, which is a bit heavier in weight and better able to handle scrapbook-style embellishing.

Another option for book pages is plain old copy paper. It's less expensive than cardstock and is perfect for memo books, where pages are used and discarded. Because copy paper is lightweight, it is easy to sew through several sheets at a time with a heavy-duty needle in your sewing machine.

> **Tip** Other materials you can consider using for your book pages (or attaching to your cardstock pages) include fabric, vellum, thin sheets of metal, acetate, and fiber mesh.

Just like fabric, paper has a grain. Cutting *with* the grain of the cardstock will allow you to make straight folds or tears much more easily. Though all paper has a grain, it is most important and visible in the heavier-weight cardstock and art paper. The easiest way to make sure you are cutting with the grain is to hold the cardstock sheet with one hand on each side and gently bend it. Then switch the sides you are holding. You should notice that one direction bends much more easily than the other. The easy bend is the direction of the grain.

✖ Fibers

I have used lots of ribbons and fibers throughout this book. They add a soft, fun, and whimsical touch to projects. My ribbons and fibers are all stored in large glass jars on a counter in my studio. That way I can always see what I have and what might work for the project at hand.

Any fiber or ribbon is fair game for decoration on books, and in my opinion, the more the merrier! I especially like old rayon and silk seam binding because of the pretty colors and the way it ties into a neat bow.

For something a little different, wire can also be a fun ribbon-like embellishment.

As binding to hold a book together, I usually use one of two types of thread or cording.

Waxed linen thread—The wax coating helps the thread stick to itself, making for a stronger knot. This thread is easy to use and comes in a variety of colors and thicknesses, or number of *plies*. (I prefer four-ply thread.)

Perle cotton cording—This cording is available in several sizes, but I like #5 the best. It is readily available at needlework stores, and if you're lucky you can sometimes find it at thrift stores or rummage sales.

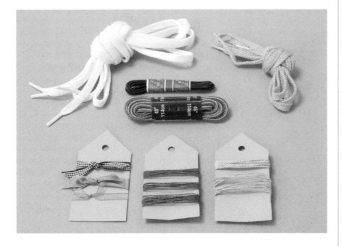

Consider using other fibers such as twines, yarns, and various ribbons. The only thing you need to keep in mind is that the fiber needs to have the strength to handle the stress of being tied in a knot strong enough to hold the book together. Test a small piece of the fiber first before the final construction of your actual book. Take the ends of your fiber firmly in both hands and pull tightly. If it breaks, it is too weak to hold your book together. This test is especially important when you are using vintage fibers!

⊠ Embellishments

You can find embellishments for your book creations just about anywhere. I am always on the lookout for something that will work in one of my books. Your perfect embellishment could just as easily be in a craft store, a thrift store, or a hardware store. Always consider an object's potential, not just the intended purpose.

There are so many wonderful treasures available in craft stores that deciding what to include on your work of art can be difficult. Let your theme be your guide. You'll have to do a little planning beforehand, but it will save you time in the long run.

Although most of the books shown here are relatively empty, I have included a few with full decoration to provide you with eye candy and inspiration.

⊠ Book Closures

While I was planning the projects to include in this book, I started noticing all the various objects that might work to keep the books closed. Some were stashed in my studio, and others are new items available in stores.

Ribbon is one of my favorite ways to close a book. You can find ribbon in many stores, and you usually have a good selection to choose from. It also can suit almost any style—it can be frilly when tied in a bow, or you can make it more traditional by adding some D-rings or a buckle to close like a belt.

Check out the hardware section in your local craft store for small latches. There are actually quite a few to choose from. In place of screws, you can use brads with just a tiny drop of glue. The scrapbook companies are also marketing various metal latches for use on books as well. These work especially well for closing the folded book covers.

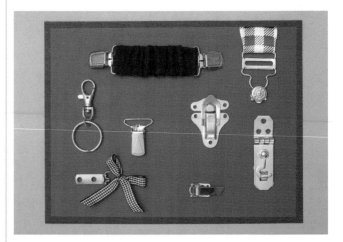

When creating a closure for your book, anything goes!

The notions department of your favorite sewing center has several offerings for you to use as book closures. Overall clasps, suspender clips, metal rings—these items can be sewn to ribbon, elastic, or even a complementary fabric to create a one-of-a-kind closure for your book.

Buttons, hook-and-loop tape, brads with reinforcements and string, pet collars, even rubber bands can be used for closures. Keep your book's theme in mind, and let your creative muse go wild!

MAKING A WRAPAROUND CLOSURE

You can also make a book closure out of fabric book cloth.

1. Cut a strip of the fabric book cloth that is ¼ as wide the height of your book and is twice as long as the width of the cover plus the depth of the book. (Just make sure your strip wraps completely around the book and meets.)

2. Wrap the strip around the entire book and trim to fit.

3. I like to trim the edge of my closures to look like the ends of tags. I use a paper tag as my guide. Once you've trimmed the edge, use a decorative stitch on your sewing machine to stitch around the entire piece.

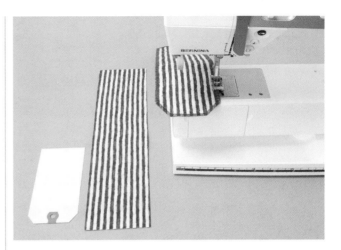

4. Punch 2 circle and 2 star shapes from cardstock, and glue a star to each circle. With a push pin, poke a hole through both embellishments and both ends of the strip, placing the embellishments about ⅜″ in from the end. Attach an embellishment to each end of the strip with a brad.

5. Finish off the closure with cording or decorative ribbon and you are good to go!

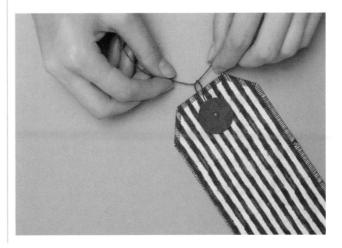

✙ Cutting Tools

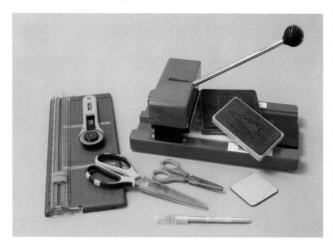

I have a large table in the center of my studio with two large, self-healing cutting mats ready for use when the creative juices start flowing. The mats—along with my clear 24″ ruler and a large rotary cutter—are what I use for cutting ordinary fabric, prepared fabric, and large art paper. The grids on my cutting mats help keep my measurements correct, and the rotary cutter is quick and easy to use. Be patient and cut only one or two sheets of paper at a time. If you stack paper, it tends to slide while you are cutting, leaving you with an unusable, angled cut.

Rotary cutter—Used by quilters for years, this circular blade is a wonder. It can cut precisely through several layers of materials at once. My studio is always set up for me to cut fabric with a rotary cutter, a clear ruler, and a self-healing cutting mat. When clearing these things away to cut paper one day, I realized I could use the same "fabric" tools for paper.

Personal paper cutter—I use this for cardstock in sizes up to 12″ x 12″. It is a neat little portable device that allows you to line up your cardstock at your designated measurements, hold it in place, and then slide the blade across the paper. These cutters come in a variety of styles and prices. The two main style differences are a rotary cut or a tear cut. I prefer the rotary cut. I find that the blade stays sharper longer, and when the blade does get dull, it simply won't cut through paper. Other styles may rip the paper when the blade gets dull.

Scissors—Scissors are still a mainstay in my studio. I have many kinds of shears for a variety of projects: thread snips; craft scissors for wire; small, fine scissors for cutting out stamped images; scissors just for paper; and, of course, scissors just for fabric. The important thing to remember is to have the correct pair of scissors for the job at hand.

Craft blade—A craft blade is another must for book projects. Together with a metal-edged ruler, it allows you to make straight, small cuts or corrections to a not-so-perfect cut. I tend to use mine to make cuts that are too small for my personal paper cutter or to cut heavier cardboard or chipboard. When cutting heavier board, I keep my knife pressure consistent and go over the cut several times, keeping the tip of the knife right along the ruler's metal edge. A good sharp knife makes this cutting task easier, so I change my blades often.

Sizzix machine—This die-cutting machine has become a favorite of mine. It is a smaller, home version of the large die-cut machines you see at your local schools and at scrapbooking stores. This tool allows you to precisely and quickly cut circles, squares, frames, letters, mini file folders, and even photo holders with a simple pull of a handle. The Sizzix machine is great for creating cardstock embellishments for your books when you don't want the added thickness that three-dimensional embellishments create.

Punches—Punches are useful for cutting basic shapes. They are easy to use and very portable. Have an assortment of graduated squares and circles on hand to make reinforcements and other embellishments for books.

Screw punch—This is my all-time favorite tool. Indispensable for skewer books, this little device allows you to drill holes wherever you want on your project. There are two types available: ratchet-style and manual. With the ratchet-style tool, all you have to do is place the tool in the spot where you want the hole and push down. This style has a variety of blades and bits available. With the manual style, you place the tool where you want your hole and then turn the tool until the hole is cut. This style has several bits in different diameters.

Hammer punch—This tool, along with a hammer, allows you to place holes in cardstock exactly where you want them. Simply place the drill over a spot where you would like a hole, and give it a little whack with the hammer. Presto! A hole!

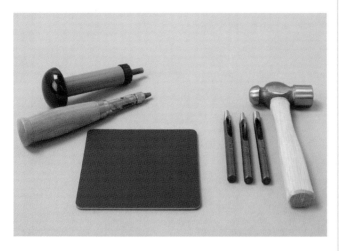

Manual punch on the left, a ratchet-style punch next, and hammer punches on the right

Drill bit sizes for screw punches start at pinpoint small and go to about ⅜ inch. When selecting a size to use, I try to remember a few things:

- Smaller is better. When adding a decorative ribbon embellishment, you don't want to see the hole the ribbon is in; you want to see only ribbon.

- Consider how many times your ribbon or thread will go through the drilled hole. If only once, keep it small. If you may go through the drilled hole a number of times, as you would with the matchbook project as you replace your memo papers, make the hole a little larger. That will prevent some of the wear and tear the holes will take when you change the ribbon.

- If you just aren't sure, make a drill-bit-gauge reference card out of a scrap of your prepared book cloth and the various drill bit sizes you have. This card will allow you to test your thread or ribbon against the hole sizes so you can select which works best.

⊠ Measuring Tools

You can't talk about cutting tools without talking about rulers. I have several sizes in the studio that I use for various purposes.

6″ × 24″ ruler—This ruler is the one I use most often with my cutting mat. It has a nice lip that fits right onto the edge of the mat—giving me extra insurance that I will make the right cut.

12″ see-through ruler—I like to use this ruler when marking the hole placement for the bindings of skewer books. The clear lines make it easy to see when I need to move things over just a smidge.

Centering ruler—A centering ruler is extremely helpful when you are tying or finishing off books. This ruler starts off with "0" in the center and is numbered out with the same measurements on each side.

Metal-edge 12″ ruler—This ruler is a must when working with a craft knife. Because the blade in your craft knife is so sharp, it could actually cut into plastic-edge rulers. The metal helps to protect you and your project.

12″-square ruler—I bought this ruler for my quilting projects so I could make sure that my quilt blocks were actually square. It also comes in handy for book covers that need to be folded. It's great for marking the areas to be cut off the covers.

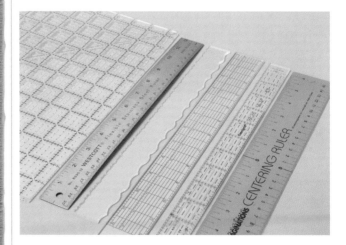

✠ Sewing Machine

You will need a sewing machine for the projects in this book. Mine has lots of fancy stitches, but a good-quality, basic machine that has only straight stitches and adjustable zigzag stitches will work just fine.

Many people are concerned about using their sewing machine to sew paper. I have not experienced any problems due to combining paper and fabric in my artwork. To keep my machine running smoothly, I clean out my bobbin area with a brush after every sewing session to prevent lint buildup. It is important to follow the manufacturer's directions for maintenance of your machine. Regular oiling and periodic checkups by a qualified sewing-machine expert will keep your machine happy for a long time!

After moving to the San Francisco Bay area, I traded in my old sewing machine and treated myself to a fancy new machine. Shortly thereafter, my new machine and I came to an agreement: if I bought only all-cotton thread, it would let me zigzag stitch—if I didn't sew too fast. Our agreement worked as long as I followed the rules.

Recently I had an opportunity to talk with an expert at one of the thread manufacturers about the agreement I had with my sewing machine. She informed me that it was my *needle* that was causing my problems, not my thread choices. She suggested I try **topstitching needles** in my machine, for all my projects. *Wow!* What a difference! These needles have a sharp point and a larger eye. This allows the thread to move through the needle without the excessive rubbing that increases the chance of breakage. I used size 12 or 14 topstitching needles for the edges of all the projects in this book and have been pleased with the results. I was even able to successfully use the pretty satin and silky threads that had tempted me for years. I still sew slowly, but now it's for accuracy, not because my thread is breaking!

✠ Adhesives

I did not use glue to put together the basic projects in this book. However, I do use a variety of adhesives when embellishing the finished books, because different embellishments require different types of glue. Here is a brief list of what I like to have available when I'm embellishing a fabric book.

Tape runners—These glue applicators are the best invention for paper crafters on the market. They are so easy to use—just run the little tool along the edge of your paper to set the glue in place. These tools come with several options: continuous glue, little tabs, permanent glue, and removable glue. The applicators and refills are a bit pricey, but for me the convenience outweighs the cost.

Fabri-Tac adhesive—This adhesive is good for gluing fabric to fabric when you won't be using an iron or other heat source on the project.

Fast-drying paper glue—This glue is great when you need to glue paper together *fast!* When using this glue, you need to move fairly quickly, but you need only a little bit.

The Ultimate!—This thick, white, tacky glue dries clear. It is easy to apply with your finger, a brush, or, my favorite, a toothpick. You need only a small amount to attach paper and cardstock to your fabric books. This glue is excellent for attaching heavy and three-dimensional embellishments such as metal letters, watchcases, and keys to fabric.

PVA glue—This glue is typically used by book artists to attach decorative papers to their book covers because it seems to minimize any warping the decorative paper may want to do. It is easy to apply with a brush, but I like to use an expired gift card or credit card or a stiff piece of cardboard to obtain thin, even coverage.

 Tip Finally, something to do with the fake credit cards that come in junk mail— use them as glue spreaders!

Xyron machine—This little hand-operated tool allows you to put adhesive on the back of ribbon, paper, vellum, or pictures, so you can glue them to your scrapbook pages or other artwork. The machine is easy to operate, and with a variety of cartridges to choose from (such as adhesive, lamination, or magnet), it makes many of your projects easy to complete.

Glue Dots—A clever inventor came up with the idea of placing consistent amounts of glue in drops on a waxy paper to peel off for use in paper crafts. These little gems are super for adhering paper and metal objects. They may be a bit tricky to use the first time; read the instructions, and don't use your fingers—that weakens the adhesive bond. The only downside I have found is that the dots seem to slide on art that is displayed vertically.

Glue sticks—I use these handy little sticks when I am going to sew paper together. A little dab between two pages is just enough to hold them together so they won't move while I'm sewing. Glue placed in the center of the pages won't be in the path of my stitches, so it won't create a mess in my sewing machine.

Diamond Glaze—I like to use this product for adding dimension or highlights to my stamped images and photographs. It goes on and dries clear. You can add dye-based inks to it for added interest.

✠ Other Tools

Here are some additional tools I use for making books:

Bone folder—A bone folder is a must for all paper and book projects. I use it to make clean folds in my cards by first scoring along the fold using a ruler as my guide and then scraping the edge of the bone folder along the paper fold to flatten it. The bone folder is also good for smoothing out paper that is being glued to another flat surface. Bone folders come in several shapes and sizes. I prefer a bone folder to an iron when making fabric book covers. The iron makes too sharp a crease, which makes adding the book's pages difficult. That doesn't mean I never use an iron; sometimes on the smaller projects an iron actually works better. Let the project guide you to which tool will work best.

Hand-sewing needles—There are two basic needles I use for finishing the fabric books. For sewing the pages to the covers or connecting the covers, I use a size 18 or 20 **tapestry needle**. I like these needles because they have a large eye, to make threading cording easy, and they are easy to manipulate through holes and eyelets. The second needle I use is a **curved needle**. It's a gem for adding fibers, ribbon, and embellishments to the spines of finished books. The needle's curve makes it so easy to slip behind the finished knots of the fibers holding your book together—this needle is a must!

Binder clips—Sometimes you need an extra hand to hold something in place while you prepare an item to glue or encourage a cover to fold in a certain way. Your typical office-supply clips (available in several sizes) will hold the embellishment or book covers in place, freeing up your hands so you can move on to the next step.

Eyelet setter and eyelets—I use these for both construction and decoration of books.

Tweezers—Tweezers are good for picking up small eyelets and stamped images or for holding paper while you are embossing.

Shank remover—Sometimes I like to use buttons as my decoration. This tool removes the back shank, making it easy to glue the button to the cover.

Wire cutters—I prefer to use wire cutters to cut wire, so that I don't nick the blade on a good pair of scissors.

Pliers—A pair of pliers comes in handy when you want to attach a jump ring to a charm—two pairs are even better!

Nonstick craft sheets—I have one or two of these sheets set up on my stamping desk all the time. Paint or stamp directly on the sheet. The Teflon allows for easy cleanup—my kind of tool!

Fray Check—Fray Check is great for preventing the holes you will drill in the book covers from fraying. It's available at your local quilt shop.

Makeup sponges—These are great tools for creating backgrounds, painting, and even adding pastel highlights.

Rubber and foam stamps—Stamps are good for adding decoration and definition to your finished books. I especially like all the new foam alphabet stamps that are so popular right now. They are available in a variety of sizes, are reasonably priced, and provide a great way to add words to your books. Put paint on your foam stamp with a foam brush for a more even look.

Foam brushes—These brushes are good for painting backgrounds onto your paper and for applying paint to foam stamps. These brushes are also great tools for removing paint from your foam stamps. Just rub the brush over your stamps under running water and the paint should come right off.

Acrylic paints and dye-based and pigment inks—I always have a variety of colors on hand because I'm never sure where creative inspiration will take me or what medium I will be stamping on.

Preparing Fabric

TWO

Book Cloth

There are several fabric adhesive products on the market, but my favorite is HeatnBond Lite Iron-On Adhesive. You can find this product at a fabric store, usually as yardage in the interfacing section or sometimes on the craft wall in packages of precut sheets. I like to purchase it as yardage and usually buy an entire bolt at a time. That way I can work not only on larger projects but also on lots of them! It's easy to use; just follow the manufacturer's directions that come with the product. HeatnBond comes in a 17-inch width but can be overlapped up to about ½ inch, which allows you to work on larger pieces of fabric or use up some HeatnBond scraps. Just be careful that you don't leave a gap in the adhesive.

For an 18″ × 22″ sheet of fabric book cloth you will need the following:

- ½ yards of 1 fabric cut in half, or 1 fat quarter each of 2 complementary fabrics (you'll need 2 pieces, roughly 18″ × 22″)

- 2 pieces of HeatnBond Lite, matching the size of your fabric pieces

- 24″ × 36″ sheet of base paper

- Iron and ironing board

- Rotary cutter and cutting mat

- Clear acrylic ruler

- Sewing machine

MAKING THE FABRIC BOOK CLOTH

1. Gather your supplies.

2. Iron the HeatnBond adhesive to the wrong side of your fabrics.

3. Let the fabric and adhesive cool. Then remove the paper backing from the adhesive and iron one of the fabric/adhesive pairs to each side of the base paper. Iron your fabrics in the same place on each side of the base paper to give you the maximum amount of fabric book cloth for your efforts.

Tip If you are using a fabric with a directional print, pay attention to the alignment of the print.

4. Once the adhesive cools, cut the prepared fabric into the desired book cover size.

5. Fold the cover in half using a bone folder or an iron.

Tip To make folding your cover easier, or if you get unwanted folds in your covers, try ironing both sides flat. Ironing warms the adhesive, removes the unwanted creases, and allows the cover to fold easily. Use your bone folder to put a new crease in place.

STITCHING AROUND THE BOOK

Once I have my cover folded and ironed to its final shape, I like to finish the cover edges with a decorative stitch. I have three favorites: the overlock, zigzag, and satin stitches. My vision of the finished book and the design of the fabric will determine the edge stitch I select. Save the scraps you generate when you cut out your covers—the size doesn't matter—and use them to practice your machine stitching. When I want a dense satin stitch, I will stitch twice around the covers for a full, rich look. Other times, as in the recipe books (page 50), a simple zigzag will work just fine. Play with your sewing machine and see which stitches work best for you. Practicing lets you experiment before you do something you don't like on your cover!

I generally use the same thread color in both the needle and bobbin. I use a size 12 or size 14 topstitching needle, and I leave the stitch-length setting alone. I try to begin my edge stitching at a fold on the book cover so that when I backstitch at the end of my stitching, it won't be quite as noticeable. For the accordion books and three-ring books with nonfolded covers, I start and stop in a corner, and instead of backstitching, I pull my cut threads through the stitching on the inside cover.

Basic Fabric Books

Three

Honey Do

I filled this book with graph paper so it's all set for home repair calculations.

Etc.

This fabric was so fun I thought it would make a whimsical note keeper by my phone.

Flower Photo Transfer

My friend Connie Baldonado loves her garden and loves to sew. What a great way to show off both!

Who Loves Ya?

My friend Krista Halligan made this very special book for her new baby girl. Each page features someone special in her daughter's life—such a keepsake!

Who Loves Ya? photo by Krista Halligan

All the following projects start with prepared

fabric book cloth you make ahead of time.

See pages 15–16 for instructions.

A three-ring book is the EASIEST book to make when you need a quick gift. It is a fun way to use up some scraps from your larger fabric books. I wanted to make a phone book for my studio (because that is where I spend most of my time), and this was a fast and fun way to make one that was both functional and decorative!

MY FRIENDS THREE-RING BOOK

Finished size: 6″ × 6¼″

SUPPLIES

- 2 pieces prepared fabric book cloth, each cut to 6″ × 6¼″ (see pages 15–16 for instructions)

- Matching thread

- 1 sheet 12″ × 12″ cardstock (or two sheets 8½″ × 11″) in each of 4 colors: lime green, blue, yellow, and orange

- Scrap of orange cardstock for cover reinforcements

- ¼″ hole and ¾″ circle punches

- 3 binder rings, 2″

- Rub-on letters: Making Memories

- Metal tabs: 7gypsies

- Glue

- Screw punch

MAKING THE BOOK

1. With your sewing machine set on a decorative stitch, stitch around the edges of the prepared fabric book cloth with matching thread. Start and stop at a corner and pull the thread tails through the stitching on the inside of the cover.

2. Cut 4 pieces, 5½″ × 5¾″, of each color of cardstock.

3. Using a screw punch, make 3 evenly spaced holes along the short side of both pieces of fabric.

4. Stack the paper and center it on the inside of the back cover. Lay the top cover on the stacked paper to use as a guide for drilling holes in the paper.

5. Drill holes.

6. Make hole reinforcements (see Making Hole Reinforcements, page 20) for the front and back cover holes from the scrap of orange cardstock, using your hole and circle punches.

7. Glue reinforcements to the front and back covers. Let the glue dry.

8. Stack the covers and paper together and attach the binder rings. Decorate the covers as desired.

MAKING HOLE REINFORCEMENTS

I like to make my own reinforcements for my books because I can make them any size and color I need them to be.

1. Start with a scrap of cardstock and punch a hole the same size as the hole you are reinforcing.

2. Center and punch out another hole in the cardstock with a hole punch ½" bigger than the first.

Note | The two hole punch sizes should be determined by one actual hole being reinforced.

Reinforcements can be added for decoration, and a little Fray Check around the holes will prevent fraying.

Tip | When you make books with separate covers, it's a good idea to drill your holes no more than ½" in from the left side of the book. If you place the holes any further in than that, the covers will not lie flat after being attached with the rings.

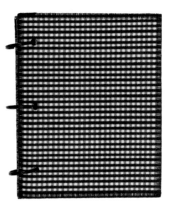

On this plain version I used split rings for the bindings.

Variation: Flower Three-Ring Book

This fun and whimsical decorated three-ring book makes a fun gift that any girl would love. Add an initial in the center of the flower for a personalized touch.

I made this book using one of those freebie junk-mail CDs as a pattern, and a spare album post I had left over from a previous project. A sharp craft knife made the cutting a breeze.

CIRCLE BOOK

Finished size: 4¾″ diameter

SUPPLIES

- A junkmail CD (or other tool that will create 4¾″ circles)

- Prepared orange fabric book cloth (see pages 15–16 for instructions), enough for 3 circles, 4¾″

- Prepared pink fabric book cloth, enough for 3 circles, 4¾″

- Prepared fuchsia fabric book cloth, enough for 2 circles, 4¾″

- Matching thread

- ¾ yard 1¼″-wide decorative ribbon

- ½″-long album post (available at scrapbooking stores)

- Screw punch

Tip Sometimes these album posts are called Chicago posts or screw-off posts. In addition to the standard aluminum, they also come in brass and black.

MAKING THE BOOK

1. Trace the CD onto the prepared fabric book cloth and cut out circles in 3 colors.

2. With your sewing machine set to a tight zigzag, stitch around the edges of each circle of prepared fabric book cloth with matching thread.

3. Stack all the fabric circles and with a screw punch drill a ¼″ hole (to match the size of the album post) ½″ in from the edge.

4. Screw the post in place and tie the ribbon in a bow around the post. The bow will hide the post.

Tip A personal die-cutting machine, such as a Sizzix, is another great way to cut shapes from fabric book cloth and cardstock.

I wanted to make a simple book that mimicked the popular accordion books found in scrapbooking and craft stores.

ACCORDION BOOK

Finished size folded: *5″ × 6″*

SUPPLIES

- Prepared fabric book cloth (see pages 15–16 for instructions), cut to 18″ × 10″

- Matching thread

- 1 yard coordinating ¾″-wide grosgrain ribbon

- Cardstock in various coordinating shades: 9 pieces 4⅜″ × 5½″; one piece 4″ × 5″

- 4 brads

- ¾ yard ½″-wide checkered ribbon

- Tacky glue

MAKING THE BOOK

1. Cut the prepared fabric book cloth into 5 rectangles, 5″ × 6″ each.

2. With your sewing machine set to a tight zigzag, stitch around the edges of each piece of prepared fabric book cloth with matching thread (see page 17).

3. Cut the grosgrain ribbon into 8 pieces, 1½″ long.

4. Lay a piece of grosgrain ribbon on a fabric book cloth rectangle 1″ from the top with the midpoint of the ribbon on the edge of the prepared fabric rectangle, so that half the ribbon is on the rectangle and half is off. Lay another piece of ribbon 1″ from the bottom.

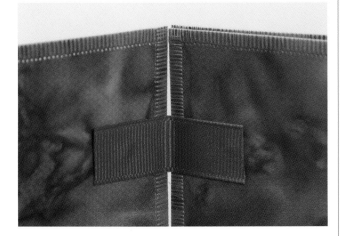

5. Stitch both pieces of ribbon to the rectangle along the inside of the previous edge stitching, so your stitching won't be too visible. A small glue dot outside the line of stitching will help hold the ribbon in place while you stitch. (The ends of the ribbon will be covered by cardstock in Step 8.)

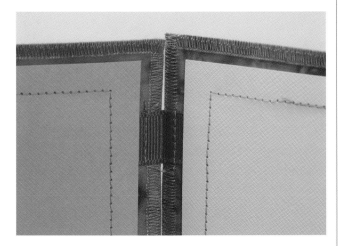

6. Line up your next prepared fabric book cloth rectangle right next to the first and sew it to the ribbon along the inside of your previous edge stitching. Repeat for the remaining 3 rectangles of fabric book cloth, alternating the ribbons from the outside to the inside.

7. Using your presser foot as your sewing guide, straight stitch ¼″ in from the edge around 8 of the 4⅜″ × 5½″ cardstock rectangles. Backstitch to hold the threads, and clip the ends close to the cardstock.

8. Run a small amount of tacky glue along the stitch line and glue cardstock to each fabric rectangle, covering the ends of the ribbon. Glue 4 cardstock pieces to the inside of the accordion book first and let the glue dry; then glue the 4 outside pieces and let the glue dry. Make sure to leave the back cover blank.

9. With your favorite adhesive, center and glue the 4″ × 5″ cardstock piece to the remaining 4⅜″ × 5½″ cardstock rectangle, then glue this to the end page of the book. This will be your front cover.

10. Add brads for decorations on the cover. You can use an awl, a pushpin, a craft knife, or a large needle to make the holes for your brads.

11. Center the checkered ribbon on the back of the accordion book and glue the ribbon in place. Leave enough ribbon on each side to tie a bow in front.

I made this assortment of coupon books to use up leftover strips of prepared fabric book cloth and paper scraps. The instructions are written for the red cat book. Once you make one of these, you'll see that you can adjust the instructions to make just about any size book. To hold the book together, I use waxed linen thread to do a "stab-style binding," explained in the instructions.

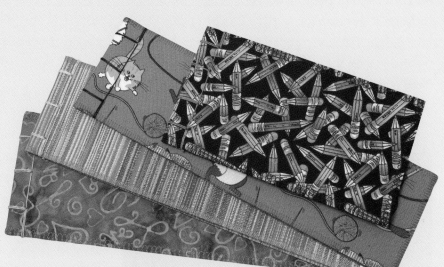

COUPON BOOK

Finished size: 3″ × 10″

SUPPLIES

- Scrap of prepared fabric book cloth, cut to 3″ × 20″ (see pages 15–16 for instructions)

- Matching thread

- Cardstock for pages

- Fabric-marking pencil

- At least 1 yard coordinating waxed linen thread

- Size 18 tapestry needle

- Screw punch

- Binder clips

MAKING THE BOOK

1. With your sewing machine set to a decorative stitch, sew around the edges of the prepared fabric book cloth with matching thread (see page 17). Remember to start and stop where a fold will be so the stitching won't be obvious.

2. Fold the cloth cover in half lengthwise and crease it with a bone folder.

3. Cut the cardstock into 8 pages, 2⅝″ × 9¾″.

4. Stack the pages and place them inside the cover against the fold, centering them from top to bottom. Use binder clips to hold the pages in the book during construction.

5. Using a fabric-marking pencil, draw a light line on the fabric cover ½″ in from the center fold. This line will help you place the holes.

6. With your screw punch, and using the pencil line as a guide, drill a small hole ½″ in from both the top and bottom of the book. Drill a third hole centered between the first 2.

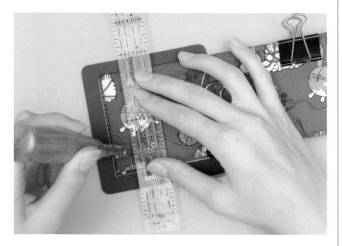

7. Thread your tapestry needle with 1 yard of waxed linen thread.

8. Temporarily remove the binder clips and open your book slightly to the center page. Bring your needle and thread through the page opening and the center book hole to the front cover, leaving a 4″ tail inside. Close the book and reclamp it.

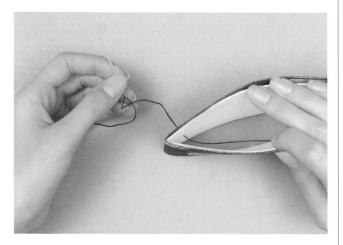

9. Wrap the thread around the spine of the book and bring the needle up through the center hole, from back to front.

10. Pull the thread through the top hole, front to back, bring the thread around the spine, and put the needle back in the same hole, pulling tight.

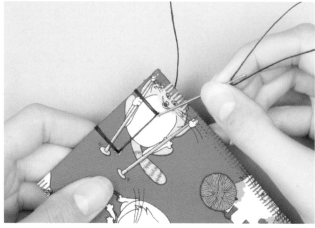

11. Wrap the thread around the spine and place the needle in the top hole a second time.

12. Bring the thread around the top of book and pull the needle through the top hole. Repeat.

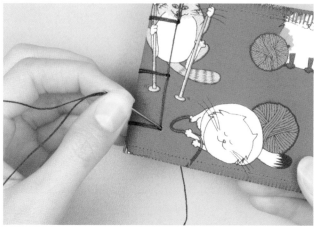

13. Bring the thread from the back cover up through the center hole to the front.

14. Take the thread from the front through the bottom hole.

15. Wrap the thread around the spine of the book twice, going through the bottom hole each time.

16. Wrap the thread around the bottom of the book twice, going through the bottom hole each time.

17. With your needle at the back of the book, remove the clamps and pull the thread through the center hole and back through to the center page, where you started to bind your book.

18. Tie the ends of the thread together and trim them to ½″.

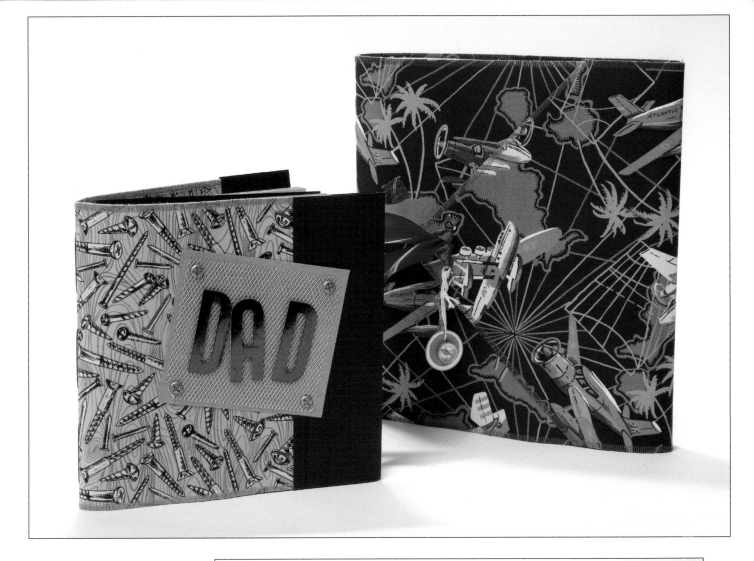

Dad Book

Here is something special for the men out there who like to work around the house. The screw fabric combines with actual hardware items to make for a fun and personalized memory book.

Blue Travel Book

For something a little different, I decided to tie the waxed linen thread to the inside of the book.

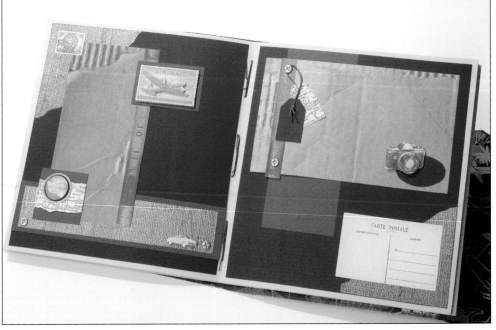

Inside page layout of Blue Travel Book

I just love making these books. They are fast, easy, and another super way to use up the long scraps of fabric book cloth I accumulate from making fabric books. I've provided basic directions for just one of the matchbooks I made. Experiment with your own scraps—these books can be just about any size.

MATCHBOOKS

Finished size: 4¼″ × 5½″

SUPPLIES

- Prepared fabric book cloth, cut to 12″ × 4¼″ (see pages 15–16 for instructions)

- Matching thread

- 2 to 4 sheets 12″ × 12″ white cardstock

- 12″ of ½″- or ⅝″-wide ribbon

- Binder clips

- Screw punch

MAKING THE BOOK

1. Cut the cardstock into 5″ × 4¼″ pieces and stack them. The exact number of pages doesn't matter; I usually use 10 to 12 pieces, which stack up to about ¼″. (This is another place to use up some scraps!)

2. With your sewing machine set to a decorative stitch, sew around the edges of the prepared fabric book cloth with matching thread (see page 17). Remember to start and stop where a fold will be so the stitching won't be obvious.

3. Fold the top of the cloth matchbook cover down 4½″, and again at 4¾″; then fold the bottom up 1½″, and again at 1¾″. Use your bone folder to make these folds sharp. The second fold allows for the thickness of the paper stack and adds a little give to the cover, just like on an actual book of matches!

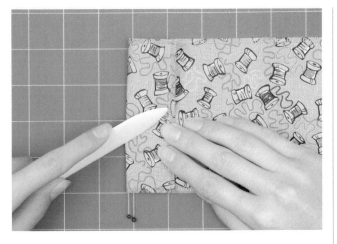

6. Thread ribbon through the holes and tie the ribbon into a bow or a knot.

4. Place the cardstock stack in the bottom fold of the book; use binder clips to hold the stack in place.

5. With your screw punch drill 2 holes, 1″ in from each side edge and ¾″ up from the bottom.

These would make great party favors, invitations, hostess gifts—the list is endless. And the best part is you can refill them again and again!

Here is yet another project for your fabric book cloth scraps. I haven't given you specific measurements—the size of the book depends on the size of your scraps.

MINI BOOKS

1. Trim a scrap of prepared fabric book cloth to the size desired (see pages 15–16 for instructions).

2. With your sewing machine set to a decorative stitch, sew around the edges of the scrap with matching thread (see page 17). Remember to start and stop where a fold will be so the stitching won't be obvious.

3. Cut cardstock pages to just ½″ smaller than the size of your cover.

4. Fold the scrap cover and the pages in half, using a bone folder to ensure a sharp crease.

5. Drill 2 holes along the spine 1″ from both the top and bottom of the book cover. (You may need more holes if you make a larger book; do what works best for you!)

6. Place the pages in the cover and drill corresponding holes in the pages.

7. Thread ribbon or cording through the holes and tie a knot or bow along the spine.

This is a quick, simple book that takes the shape of the ever-popular tag.

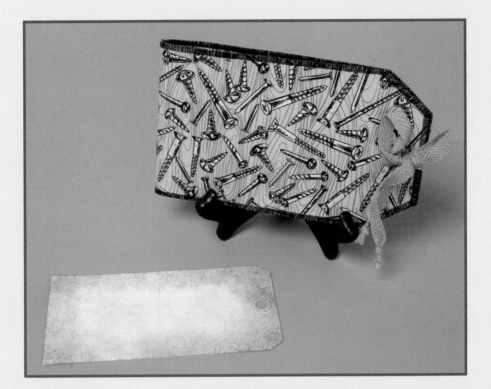

TAG BOOK

Finished size: 7¾″ × 4½″

SUPPLIES

- Prepared fabric book cloth, cut to 15½″ × 4½″ (see pages 15–16 for instructions)
- Matching thread
- 5 sheets 12″ × 12″ coordinating cardstock
- Size 18 tapestry needle
- Waxed linen thread, or other cording
- At least a yard of ½″-wide ribbon
- Embellishments
- Paper tag to use as pattern
- Screw punch

MAKING THE BOOK

1. Using an actual tag as your pattern, trim both ends of the prepared fabric book cloth to match the top of the tag.

2. With your sewing machine set to a decorative stitch, sew around the edges of the prepared fabric book cloth with matching thread (see page 17). Remember to start and stop where a fold will be so the stitching won't be obvious.

3. Fold the cloth cover in half using a bone folder to make a sharp crease.

4. Drill a hole in the middle of the tag book, so that it looks like an actual tag.

5. Cut your cardstock into 10 pages, 12″ × 4½″.

6. Fold the cardstock in half lengthwise.

7. Stack pages inside cover, fold, and clamp them together.

8. Using a screw punch, drill 4 holes along the spine of the book ¾″ in from both the top and bottom, and again 1¾″ in from the top and bottom of the cover.

9. Thread a size 18 tapestry needle with waxed linen thread or other cording, loop the thread through the top 2 holes, and tie it along the inside of the spine. Repeat for the remaining 2 holes.

10. Loop ribbon through the holes at the top of the tag to close the book, and embellish as desired. I used actual hardware washers as fun reinforcements for the nuts and bolts book.

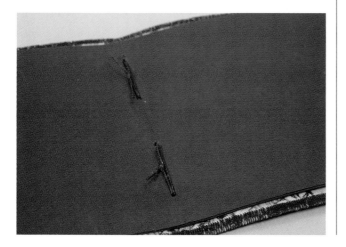

Chicken Scratch

Here's another fun version of the tag book. This is another case of the fabric telling me what to do!

I love to collect vintage photos; the faces, the clothing, and the muted shades inspire me. I got the idea for this book from the wonderful vintage photo holders that accompanied the old black-and-white or sepia photos. The covers are almost as beautiful and interesting as the photos themselves.

PAPER BAG POCKETS BOOK

Finished size: 8″ × 5¼″

SUPPLIES

- Prepared fabric book cloth, cut to 21¼″ × 5¼″ (see pages 15–16 for instructions)

- Matching thread

- 1 strip dark brown cardstock, 1½″ × 12″

- 1 strip light brown cardstock, 1″ × 12″

- 6 brown kraft bags, wine-bottle size

- 4 eyelets and eyelet setter

- Brown waxed linen thread

- Size 18 or size 20 tapestry needle

- Screw punch

- Assorted snaps or brads

- Embellishments

MAKING THE BOOK

1. If desired, trim one end of the prepared fabric book cloth into a point, to tuck into the loop closure. With your sewing machine set to a decorative stitch, stitch around the edges of the prepared fabric book cloth (see page 17) with matching thread. Remember to start and stop where a fold will be so the stitching won't be obvious.

2. With the inside of the cloth cover facing you, fold the cover over 7¼″ from the left side. Crease with a bone folder.

3. Using your screw punch, drill 4 evenly spaced holes along the fold on the cover: 2 holes 1″ from the top and bottom and another 2 holes 2¼″ from the top and bottom.

4. Set an eyelet in each hole in the book cover, with the finished side of the eyelet on the outside of the cover.

5. Cut off the tops and bottoms of each paper bag to obtain six 13½″ tubes.

6. Fold the paper bags in half crosswise.

7. Referring to Step 3, drill 4 holes along the folds in the bags to correspond with the holes in the cover.

8. Starting inside the book, with a tapestry needle and waxed linen thread, loop the thread through the top 2 holes twice and end inside the book. Make sure to leave long enough tails so you can tie the ends into a knot, holding the bags in place. Repeat for the bottom 2 holes along the fold in the book.

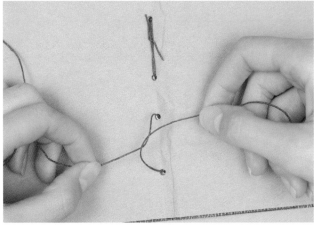

Some treasures I tucked into a pocket of the book

SETTING AN EYELET

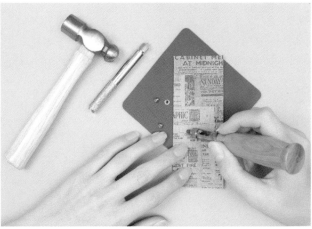

1. Drill a hole in the fabric paper where the eyelet is to be placed.

2. Place the setter in the back of the eyelet and strike it with a hammer. Make sure you are working on a hard surface to ensure a smooth set. Don't worry if the back of the eyelet doesn't look pretty; it usually cannot be seen. As long as your eyelet is secure in place you are good to go!

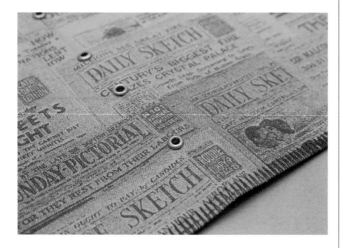

MAKING THE LOOP CLOSURE

1. Center the light brown cardstock on the dark brown cardstock and glue together.

2. Place the layered cardstock on the cover flap of the book.

3. Fold the end of the layered cardstock closure inside the cover. Leave a little room for the second cover to slide through. Crease the fold.

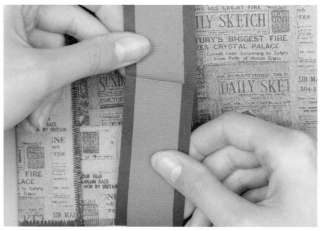

4. Embellish the front of the cardstock strip and glue the ends together. Fold the right cover over and tuck it into the loop.

Tip After I had cut out this book, stitched around all the edges, and added my paper bags, I discovered that the left cover was too long. Instead of starting all over, I decided to add a pocket on the left inside flap, stitched down as in the *Teacher's Book* (page 53). To make it look like I had planned this pocket all along, I added a couple of tags and an optical lens to better view the treasures inside the book. No one will ever know!

This book is a variation on the vintage photo cover idea. Just to be different, I came up with a unique way to add the pages. I wanted this to be feminine and girly, so I added ribbon and tied lots of bows.

MOM'S CHECKERED PINK BOOK

Finished size: 8¼″ × 8¼″

SUPPLIES

- Prepared fabric book cloth, cut to 20″ × 8¼″ (see pages 15–16 for instructions)

- Matching thread

- 12 pieces light pink textured cardstock, 6½″ × 7½″

- 8 pieces dark pink textured cardstock:

  6 pieces 4″ × 7½″ (A)

  1 piece 7¼″ × 7¾″ (B) for front of book

  1 piece 3″ × 6″ (C) for back of book

- Pink 5mm perle cotton

- At least 1 yard of 1½″-wide double-faced cream satin ribbon

- 4 pink brads: Lasting Impressions

- 6 pieces assorted ribbon, each about ½″ wide by 23″ long

- Adhesive

- Clear-drying glue

- Screw punch

MAKING THE BOOK

1. Trim a front flap, using a shape you desire.

2. With your sewing machine set to a decorative stitch, stitch around the edges of the prepared fabric book cloth (see page 17) with matching thread.

3. Fold the left half of the cover over 8″. Use your bone folder to make a sharp crease. Fold right edge over 3¾″ for flap.

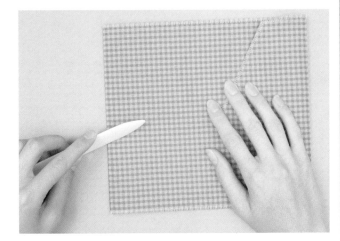

4. Take 2 pieces of light pink cardstock, textured side out, and sew them together along one short edge with a straight stitch, using your presser foot as your seam allowance guide. Repeat for the remaining 5 light pink pairs.

Tip

Paper clips or a small amount of adhesive will help hold the cardstock in place while you sew. Just make sure not to put your adhesive in the line of your sewing.

5. Fold the 6 A pieces of dark pink cardstock in half so they measure 2″ × 7½″.

6. Drill ⅛″ holes along the fold of each A piece of dark pink cardstock, ½″ from both the top and bottom.

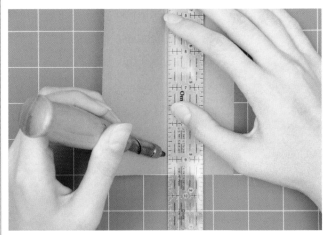

7. String a 15″ length of perle cotton through the holes so the ends are outside the fold.

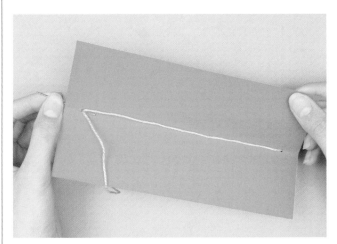

8. Using your favorite adhesive, lightly glue a sewn light pink cardstock pair into a fold of a dark pink cardstock A piece, overlapping by ⅝″, with the sewn edge of the light pink pages toward the bottom. Repeat for the remaining 5 pages. Sew the pages in place, stitching along the edge of the dark pink cardstock through all 4 layers.

9. Add pieces of the ½″-wide assorted ribbons around each page as desired for decoration, tied in a knot or bow.

10. Drill 2 holes ½″ apart along the left fold of the book cover, ¾″ from the top and bottom edges.

11. Lay the pages in the book, threading 3 ends of perle cotton through each of the left cover holes and 3 ends through each of the right cover holes. Tie the perle cotton ends together in a knot on the front. Add a drop of clear-drying glue for security.

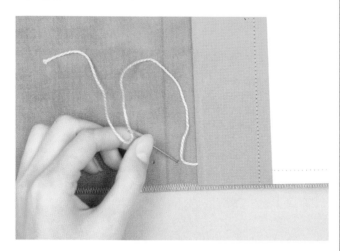

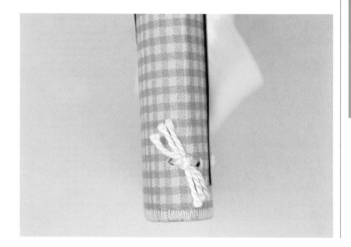

12. For cover: On the B piece of dark pink cardstock, straight stitch around the edge of the cardstock using your presser foot as your guide.

13. Place a pink brad in each corner of your stitching. Adhere the brads to the front with a very small amount of glue.

14. Lay the satin ribbon across the back of the book. On top of the ribbon, place the C piece of dark pink cardstock and sew ⅛″ in from the 2 longest edges. (I did it this way so I wouldn't have to thread my ribbon through the sleeve after sewing it to the cover.)

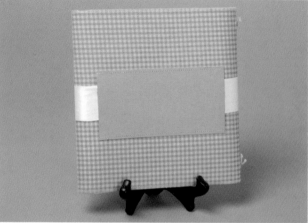

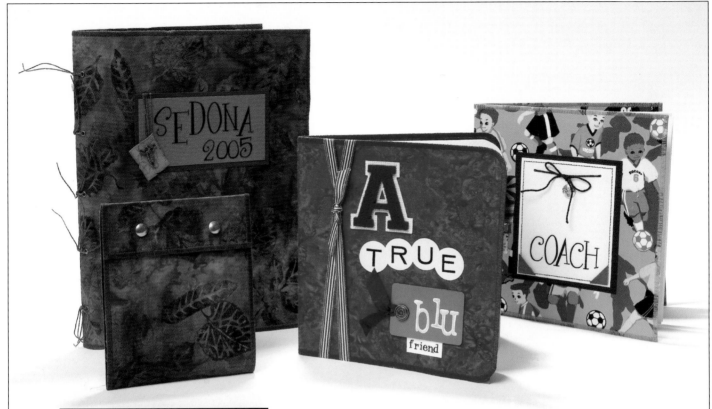

Sedona Memory

Friends were going to spend their family vacation in Sedona, Arizona, and I thought their trip was a great opportunity to use one of the patterns in the book to make a special photo keepsake for them. As a little extra, I made a coordinating matchbook for them to take along so that Mom could keep track of all the little happenings that make for a special family vacation!

A True Blu Friend

For an alternative to square corners, try rounding the corners of your book. I used a CD, but you could use a glass or a plate to get a pleasing result.

Thank You, Coach!

There are so many wonderful sports-related fabrics on the market that you could make this book for almost any coach (or player) as a remembrance of a great season or career.

Carousel Book

My friend Terrece, an avid stamp artist, was very willing to create one of my book patterns—especially because she was able to feature some of her treasured stamps!

Christmas Memories

This is a fast and fun holiday gift for family or friends. Instead of individual pages, I chose to make accordion-style pages. It's fun to see how the various covers, page styles, and bindings work together!

Here's a fun activity book for that special someone (of any age!) who likes playing with dolls.

PARIS PAPER DOLL BOOK

Finished size: 15″ × 9″

I made this book with handles so it can be carried like a briefcase.

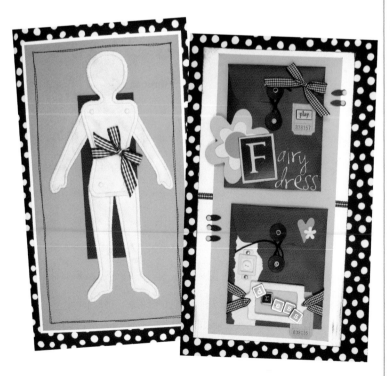

SUPPLIES FOR BASIC BOOK

- Prepared fabric book cloth (see pages 15–16 for instructions)

  Cover cut to 15″ × 18″

  4 pages cut to 14″ × 18″

- 26″ of black-and-white striped 2″-wide ribbon

- Matching thread

SUPPLIES FOR DOLL

- 1 piece, 6″ × 8″, of fast2fuse: C&T Publishing

- 2 pieces, 6″ × 8″, of all-cotton fabric

- Matching thread

- Chalk pencil

- Paper doll: Really Big Spirit Doll stamp: Limited Edition (see Sources, page 62)

- 4 complementary color brads: Lasting Impressions

SUPPLIES FOR DECORATING INSIDE OF BOOK

- Cardstock in assorted colors: Bazzill Basics

- Envelopes: Li'l Davis Designs

- Rub-on letters and words, brads, metal letters: Making Memories

- Rub-on backgrounds: Distressed Effects by My Mind's Eye

- Die cuts from Sizzix machine

- Black photo holders: Junkitz

- Assorted tags: American Tag

- Metal letters: Colorbök

- Pink label frame: K&Company

- Large letter stickers: Wordsworth

- Cat: Hirschberg Schutz & Co.

- Sandpaper: I snuck this out of the garage!

MAKING THE BOOK

1. With your sewing machine set to a decorative stitch, sew around the edges of the prepared fabric book cloth with matching thread (see page 17). Remember to start and stop where a fold will be so the stitching won't be obvious. Repeat for all 4 fabric pages.

2. Fold the cloth cover in half to 15″ × 9″ and the pages to 14″ × 9″, using a bone folder to ensure a sharp crease.

3. Mark the inside center of the book cover and pages with a chalk pencil.

4. Sew 1 page to the cover, lining up the fold of the page to the chalk line on the cover. Sew along the fold of the page, just to the left of the chalk line on the cover, and then sew a second page just to the right of the chalk line on the cover. Clamp the page to the cover to hold it in place while sewing them together on the machine.

Tip I wanted to make this book like a purse or briefcase. I sewed 13″ of ribbon to the outside edge of the book, one end 5″ from the top of the book and the other end 5″ from the bottom. I overlapped the ribbon and the book edges by about 1½″, and did the same for the opposite outside cover. To cover the raw edges of my ribbon, I used a leftover piece of cardstock from the inside pages, trimming it and then sewing it in place.

MAKING THE DOLL

1. Fuse one piece of 6″ × 8″ fabric to each side of the fast2fuse, following the manufacturer's directions.

2. Stamp the paper doll onto cardstock to make a template and then cut out and trace the pattern onto the fabric-covered fast2fuse.

3. Cut out the doll pieces.

4. With your sewing machine set to a tight zigzag, stitch around the edges of each piece of the paper doll with matching thread (see page 17).

5. Put the body parts together with brads at the shoulders and hips.

6. You can leave your doll plain, or you can paint, stamp, or otherwise embellish her.

DECORATING THE BOOK

All the scenes in the book were created freehand with simple shapes. Follow the photos if you want to follow my pattern.

Let your imagination go wild when you decorate the envelopes for your doll's clothes. I used whatever embellishments I could find in my studio and kept adding treasures, even after I thought I was finished.

 **Tip** I discovered that some (but not all) 18-inch doll clothes fit the paper doll, so that is what is tucked into in the clothing envelopes!

Variations:

- Use an actual paper doll and her accessories (or draw your own!) to include on the pages.

- What about a puzzle book? Add 2-prong fasteners to the pages with various kinds of puzzles attached, like crosswords, word jumbles, and sudoku puzzles. Make spots for pens, pencils, erasers, and a sharpener, too.

- Travel games would be another fun book. Use your computer to print out various games for everyone to play while riding in a car.

- Whether it's baseball cards or artist trading cards, you can make a fun, themed book to keep them all safe and visible!

This book is a breeze to make, thanks to the wonderful fabric paper created by Michael Miller.

FABRIC PAPER PAGES BOOK

Finished size: 6¾″ × 6¾″

SUPPLIES

- Prepared fabric book cloth, cut to 6¾″ × 13½″ (see pages 15–16 for instructions)

- Matching thread

- 4 sheets coordinating Michael Miller fabric paper

- 2 pieces, ¾ yard long, of ½″-wide coordinating ribbon

- Binder clips

MAKING THE BOOK

1. With your sewing machine set to a tight zigzag, stitch around the edges of the prepared fabric book cloth with matching thread (see page XX for instructions).

2. Fold the cloth cover in half and crease it with a bone folder.

3. Cut each sheet of fabric paper into 2 pieces, 11¾″ × 6″.

4. Place 2 matching fabric paper pieces wrong sides together, one on top of the other. Using your sewing machine, straight stitch ¼″ in around the edge of the fabric paper pair. Repeat for the remaining 3 pairs.

5. Fold the sewn pairs in half with your bone folder, matching the short ends.

6. Stack 2 unfolded fabric paper pairs together on top of the cover, matching the folds. Using a binder clip to hold the pages in place, sew them to the cover along the fold. Make sure to backstitch at the beginning and end of your stitching to lock your seam in place.

7. Place the next folded fabric paper pair between the front cover and the previously sewn pairs. Sew in place along the fold. Repeat for the last fabric paper pair, placing this remaining pair between the first sewn pair and the back cover.

8. Using the photo as a guide, tie 2 ribbons around the center of the book, adding charms and embellishments as desired.

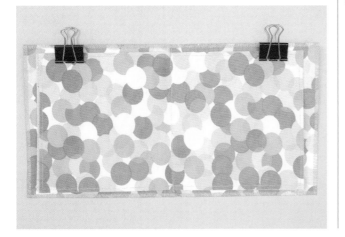

One of the most popular quilts from my *Fast, Fun & Easy Scrapbook Quilts* book was the quilt about my scouting experiences. It seems that most people have a memory or at least a good story to tell about their time in scouts. So I thought including a book for all the scouting enthusiasts out there as a place to write down all those good stories, maybe even adding a few pictures, was the right thing to do. Why, this book would make a great troop activity!

SCOUTING MEMORY BOOK

Finished size: 8″ × 10¼″

SUPPLIES

- Prepared fabric book cloth (see pages 15–16 for instructions)

  Cover cut to 8″ × 20½″

  3 strips cut to 7¾″ × 3⅝″

- Matching thread

- 12 sheets 12″ × 12″ tan textured cardstock

- 1 to 2 sheets 12″ × 12″ green textured cardstock

- 18 gold Fleur d'Lis brads: Creative Impressions

- Scouting chipboard letters: Making Memories

- Screw punch

- Cutting mat

- Chalk pencil

MAKING THE BOOK

1. With your sewing machine set to a decorative stitch, sew around the edges of the prepared fabric book cloth pieces with matching thread. Remember to start and stop where a fold will be so the stitching won't be obvious.

2. Fold the cloth cover and the 3 strips in half and crease them using a bone folder.

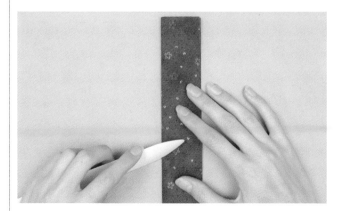

3. Using a straight stitch, sew one folded strip along the inside fold of the book cover—don't forget to backstitch to lock the seam in place. Draw a line with a chalk pencil to help you sew a straight line.

4. Sew the 2 remaining folded strips along either side of the first sewn strip.

5. Cut your tan cardstock into 12 rectangles, 7½″ × 9″, and glue 2 rectangles together, one on top of the other, with the textured sides out. Glue the remaining 5 sets together.

 When you are drilling holes in your fabric strips and your cardstock pages, place a protective mat under the strips and the cardstock to prevent unwanted holes in your covers!

6. Using a screw punch with a small bit (⅟₁₆″) and a protective cutting mat, drill 3 evenly spaced holes ⅜″ in from the edge of the fabric strips inside the book.

7. Place 1 piece of your layered cardstock under a drilled strip, centering from top to bottom and with a 1″ overlap. Using the holes already in the fabric strips as your guide, drill holes in the cardstock. Repeat for the remaining cardstock pages.

 If you have trouble aligning your cardstock on the fabric strips, a tiny bit of your favorite adhesive or a set of clamps should help hold it in place while you drill.

8. Add decorative brads in the drilled holes to keep the cardstock attached to the fabric strips.

9. Cut green cardstock into 6 pieces, 2″ × 7″. Glue 1 piece to the backside of each tan cardstock page for a decorative element and, more importantly, to cover the prongs of the brads.

10. Decorate the cover using scraps of leftover cardstock and chipboard letters.

Skewer Books

Four

Dream Book

When I saw this fabric, the theme came to mind immediately. Isn't this the perfect place to write down your dreams?

Love Book

Here is an example of a book created without any pictures— just lots of embellishments, heart charms, ribbons, and fun!

Wine Book

This book made its first appearance in Spectacular Cards. I want to show it again because of the embellishments I added. I glued small eyelet screws into each cork so I could tie them to the book's spine. It's the perfect finishing touch, don't you think?

Are We There Yet? Book

I made this book as a place to keep treasures from a spontaneous vacation my friend Jois and I took up the California coast a couple of summers ago. The wheel embellishment was the perfect finishing touch.

Who would have thought you could take a couple of little wooden sticks, some fabric, adhesive, paper, and cardstock, and come up with one-of-a-kind books to match just about any occasion? Just follow along and find out how easy it can be.

This is the book project that started it all. The fabric was fun, and I loved selecting the bright colors for the pages. In this project, you'll learn the basic construction techniques for all the skewer book projects in this book.

FRIENDS BOOK

Finished size: *6″ × 6″*

SUPPLIES

- 2 prepared fabric book cloth covers, each cut to 6″ × 12″ (see pages 15–16 for instructions)

- Cardstock (I used purple, lime green, and orange) cut into 2 each of the following sizes:

    4½″ × 10½″   5″ × 11″   5½″ × 11½″

- Large-eyed needle

- Screw punch

- Assorted paper tags, trims, fibers, ribbons, and charms from your stash

- Metal photo corners, washers, letters, safety pins, brads, and rub-on letters: Making Memories

- Sticker letters: Provo Craft

- 2 double-pointed, 6″-long knitting needles

- 4 yards of orange perle cotton cording

MAKING THE BOOK

1. With your sewing machine set to a decorative stitch, sew around the edges of the prepared fabric book cloth pieces with matching thread (see page 17). Remember to start and stop where a fold will be so the stitching won't be obvious.

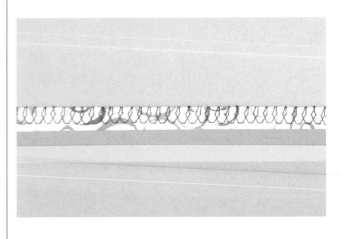

2. After folding the cloth covers and the cardstock pieces in half, matching the short ends, unfold them and layer your covers and cardstock into 2 similar stacks and drill 4 evenly spaced holes down the center of each fold.

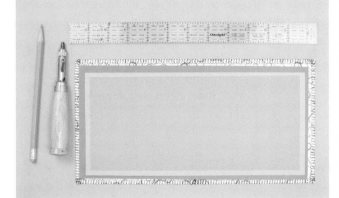

3. Using a large-eyed tapestry needle, thread cording through 1 hole from the outside of 1 of the paper and fabric stacks. Lay a double-pointed knitting needle along the fold.

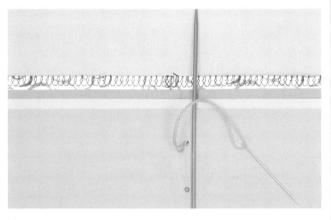

4. Wrap the cording around the knitting needle twice and come back out the same hole.

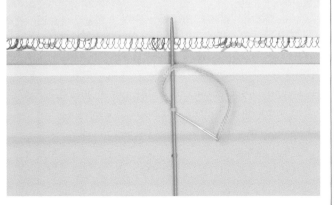

5. Take your large-eyed needle and cording through the corresponding hole on the second stack of paper and fabric. Lay the second knitting needle in the fold and wrap the cording around the knitting needle twice and come back out the same hole.

6. Tie the cording ends together in a knot. You can trim off the ties, or you can leave them long and add charms and embellishments to them from the outside of your book. Repeat for the remaining 3 holes.

7. Decorate the inside of your book with the embellishments of your choice.

MAKING A POCKET
FOR YOUR TREASURES

1. Sew approximately a presser foot's width away from the edge of the 2 center fabric pages, along the bottom and up the side of the outer edge of the page, leaving 1½″ along the side and the top unsewn.

2. To finish your pocket, fold over the unsewn corner and secure with scraps of decorative cardstock and a brad (I painted mine). If you don't have a decorative brad, you could also use ribbon. Just drill 2 holes, thread the ribbon through both holes, and then tie a knot or a bow.

Tip When placing a brad or ribbon closure on the pocket, you will need to use a screw punch to drill the holes. Remember to place a protective cutting mat inside the pocket so you don't put any holes all the way through your book!

Variations: Recipe Books

Here are a couple of variations of the *Friends Book*. *Good Eats* is for my girlfriend's daughter, who is heading off to college and dorm life. Cooking for herself will be a new experience for her, so I gathered recipes from her friends and family to create this beautiful book for her to take to school. What a great way to share something useful and so full of love!

To decorate the spine of the book, I looped small lengths of ribbon around the cord used to tie the book together.

I use a curved needle to make this looping process a lot easier. You can add just a few ribbons or a whole bunch—either way it is a fun finishing touch to the book.

On the left is the *Let's Eat!* recipe book. I had recipes scattered all over the place, in drawers, as placeholders in cookbooks—the system just wasn't working, so I made this book to keep the recipes together. The fabric was perfect for all my Italian dishes!

Tip Skewer books do not have to be square. The finished size of *Let's Eat!* is 7¾″ × 6¼″.

Skewer books can definitely come in a variety of sizes. This is another great way to use up scraps. The skewers are painted toothpicks for this little one!

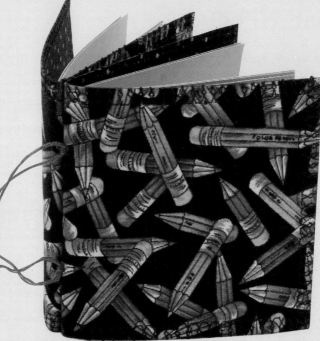

PENCIL MINI BOOK

Finished size: 3¼″ × 3¼″

SUPPLIES

- 2 pieces prepared fabric book cloth (mine are cut to 3¼″ × 6½″)

- 8 pieces complementary colored cardstock, ½″ smaller than the fabric book cloth covers (mine are cut to 3″ × 6″)

- 2 toothpicks painted in a complementary color

- 1 yard red waxed linen thread

- Screw punch

 Tip Not only are little books quick to make, but you can get rid of scraps in various sizes. Any piece of fabric book cloth large enough to fold and hold its shape will work—simply follow the directions using whatever scraps you have available!

MAKING THE BOOK

1. Cut your fabric book cloth and paper scraps to your desired size. With your sewing machine set to a decorative stitch, stitch around the prepared fabric cloth with matching thread.

2. Fold the covers using your bone folder or iron, and fold the pages in half.

3. Drill a couple of holes along the spine of each cover, about ½″ in from the spine edge at the top and bottom.

4. Center the cardstock book pages, and clamp them to the covers. Using the holes in the covers as guides, drill holes in the cardstock.

5. Follow the directions on pages 48–49 to finish construction of the book, using the toothpicks in place of the knitting needles.

It's quick and easy. These little books make great party favors, gift tags, and notebooks for your purse. Kids love them because they can be just the right size for their little hands. If you are like me, you will start buying fabric just to make these precious little books and not limit yourself to your scraps!

Once you start making small skewer books you won t want to stop.

Skewers and Needles

When I started making skewer books, I used the bamboo skewers I found in the cooking section of my grocery store. They are easy to find, easy to cut to size, and easy to paint. All great—but I wondered what else I could use. I realized I could use anything as a skewer as long as it was fairly cylindrical and not too large in diameter. Then I discovered double-pointed knitting needles. They work great! I started collecting them before the knitting craze started. Now they are getting a bit more difficult to find, and definitely cost more!

For some of my special theme books, I like to use a skewer that relates to the overall theme of the book. Pencils, paintbrushes, chopsticks, even swizzle sticks can be great and whimsical additions to your books. But there are a couple of things to watch out for:

- Sometimes using a tapered or a large-diameter skewer can change the finished look of a book. Try using paintbrushes as skewers. Paintbrushes are slightly tapered, and therefore the covers of the finished book are slightly angled. I was able to partially correct for this by inserting a pocket variation, and I liked the look of the paintbrush, so I was willing to live with the results.

- If you add a large skewer to a single-cover book, the skewer may take up a lot of space and push some of the pages out beyond the covers. To solve this problem, trim the pages to fit after the book is constructed.

- When you make a skewer book with 2 fabric covers, a large skewer can push the part of the covers in the middle of the book out beyond the front and back covers. When this happens, I usually modify my center pocket so that this is no longer an issue (see the *Teacher's Book*, page 53).

- If you don't want to include a pocket, you can change the fold line in your covers. Move the front cover fold line ¼" to the right and the back cover fold line ¼" to the left. This modification will help to make your book covers come out even. Alter this measurement depending on what size skewer you use. Test on a practice piece first.

- Your books will grow as you add treasures to them— the more you add the wider the book will become, taking up more cover space and pushing the pages out beyond the cover. If you want to avoid this, add an inch to your cover width dimensions when you first cut out your book covers. Leave the page dimensions alone. This will create a bit of give in the covers.

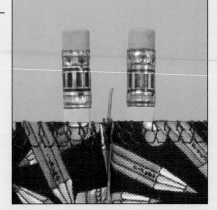

I'm always trying to create something special and a little different for the teachers I know. As if this fabric wasn't cute enough by itself, I decided to use pencils as my skewers and add a report card for a bit of whimsy.

TEACHER'S BOOK

Finished size: 6½″ × 6½″

SUPPLIES

- 2 pieces prepared fabric book cloth, each cut to 6½″ × 13″ (see pages 15–16 for instructions)

- Matching thread

- 2 sheets 12″ × 12″ black cardstock

- 2 pencils (instead of skewers!)

- 4 yards red crochet cotton

- 1–2 yards vintage red seam binding

- Charms and tags for embellishments

- 2 small black clamps

- Report card: 7gypsies

- Mini globe embellishment (This one came from a pair of garage-sale earrings!)

- Screw punch

- Scrap of string

MAKING THE BOOK

1. With your sewing machine set to a decorative stitch, sew around the edges of both pieces of the prepared fabric book cloth with matching thread. Remember to start and stop where a fold will be so the stitching won't be obvious.

2. Cut 4 cardstock pages, 6″ × 12″.

3. With the screw punch, drill 4 evenly spaced holes along the spine of the cardstock and the cloth book covers.

4. Follow the directions on pages 48–49 to construct the book using pencils as skewers and red crochet cotton for the ties.

5. Decorate the spine with red seam binding, adding charms and tags as desired.

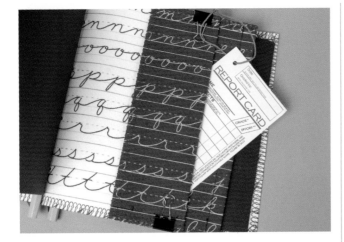

MAKING THE CENTER POCKET

1. On the first center fabric book page, fold 2¼″ toward the front, and then straight stitch along the top and bottom, close to your decorative stitching, making a pocket.

2. On the second center fabric book page, fold 1″ over toward the back, and then stitch down along the edge of the page, a presser-foot's distance away from the edge.

3. Using the small black clamps, clamp the 2 pages together. This makes a pocket for the report card.

4. Punch a hole in the report card and attach the card to the clamp with the scrap of string.

Embellishment Variations:

- Paint a small piece of chipboard with chalkboard paint and write the teacher's name in chalk.

- Don't forget an apple for teacher! Keep your eyes open for an apple or teacher-related necklace or pin—you can find fun, inexpensive jewelry at thrift shops, garage sales, and bazaars. These make great add-ons to your finished book!

Dragonfly Book
My friend Margaret Rodgers loves dragonflies and has been collecting embellishments for quite a while. When I asked her to make a book, she was off and running. What a great place to keep her winged friends!

Two Spoiled Cats Book
We love our cats dearly and wanted a place to keep all the I can t believe they did that! photos we have collected over the years.

Heritage Book

This book is for my friend. She loves almost anything vintage, especially old sewing things. I made this book so she would have a place to keep her sewing treasures. I added thimbles to the spine by using a hammer and a nail to create a small hole in the top of each thimble to slip a knotted thread through.

Beach Book

What a fun book for Grandma! She can add photos of the grandkids and all her friends!

Reindeer Book

This book started out as a pair of boxer shorts that had been a gift but were too small. My girlfriend loves the spirit of the reindeer, so I had to come up with a way to put the fabric to use. Why, a book, naturally!

Terrece s Doghouse

My friend Terrece wanted to make her dog Angel a book about all of Angel s friends. What a good mom!

Folded Books

Five

A Family That Plays Together Stays Together Book

My friend Carrie made this book as a keepsake of all the fun times her family has had playing cards. Although she made it with her parents in mind, she just might keep it for herself!

Flower Girl

Here's something fun for that girly girl in your life.

Folded Blue Stripe

My friend Vanessa made this for the man in her life. She started to add lots of fun masculine embellishments, but he said to stop so she did!

I love the anticipation when opening a present. First the tag, the ribbon, and the paper, then opening the box ... ever ... so ... slowly. The folded book carries that joy of anticipation. With various cardstock and embellishments, you, as the artist, can create a similar sense of wonder and pleasure each time someone folds a part of the cover back. I'll show you the basics ... you can take it from there to wherever you want to go!

I like to use lots of ribbon and tie lots of bows. My friends tease me constantly that I would put a bow (or two!) on every one of my creations if they didn't convince me to try something else every now and again. Here is a book with a couple of different closures to truly prove I can leave the bows off—once in awhile!

BASIC FOLDED BOOK

Finished size: 9½″ × 6¾″

SUPPLIES

- Prepared fabric book cloth, cut to 22″ × 14″ (see pages 15–16 for instructions)

- Matching thread

- 10 pieces 6″ × 9″ green cardstock

- 2 brads

These little closures, which used to be found only at office-supply stores, can now be purchased at scrapbooking stores in lots of fun patterns and colors!

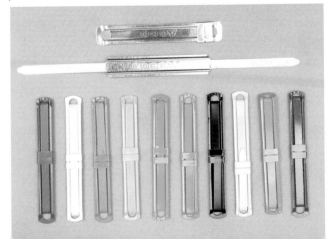

- Red and yellow cardstock scraps for circle reinforcements

- ⅜″ and ⅞″ circle punches

- One piece chipboard, 5¾″ × 8¾″

- 15″ length of red waxed linen thread

- Adhesive

- 2-prong fastener

- Screw punch

MAKING THE BOOK

1. This book has side covers that fold in and meet in the middle before the top and bottom covers overlap on the outside. Decide which is the top of your prepared fabric book cloth. For the fabric on the front covers to be right side up, the back of the book and the side covers will appear upside down.

2. Cut away a 3⅝″ × 8″ rectangle from each bottom corner.

3. Cut away a 3⅝″ × 4½″ rectangle from each top corner.

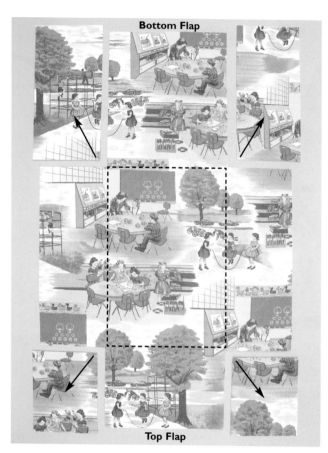

Arrows represent cutaways; dashed lines are fold lines.

4. With your sewing machine set to a decorative stitch, sew around the edges of the cloth cover with matching thread (see page 17). Remember to start and stop where a fold will be so the stitching won't be obvious.

Tip This is one of those instances I wish I hadn't used a directional fabric for my book. Fortunately the covers folded so that it looks like I planned it very carefully.

5. Make folds in the book, on the top and the bottom and both sides. Use your bone folder to ensure sharp creases.

6. Stack your green cardstock into 5 sets of 2 sheets each.

7. Trim 2″ off 1 end of 2 of the sheets. Trim 1½″ off the second set of 2 sheets, 1″ off the third set, ½″ off the fourth set, and then leave the fifth set of 2 sheets uncut. Stack these together, with the largest sheets on the bottom, up to the smallest sheets on top. Align the pages so that the top of the sheets is flush and the bottom is staggered.

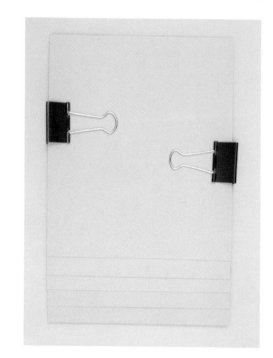

8. With your favorite adhesive, glue the chipboard to the bottom sheet of cardstock for support.

9. Along the flush (top) edge of your cardstock stack, center the top of your 2-prong fastener even on each side and ½″ down from the top edge. Make pencil marks through the holes in the top part of the fastener so you know where to drill your holes. With your screw punch, drill 2 holes at the pencil marks all the way through the cardstock stack and the chipboard.

10. Lay your cardstock stack on your fabric and drill corresponding holes in the fabric cover.

11. Coming from the back of the book, insert the bottom of the 2-prong fastener through the cover and all the sheets of cardstock (and the chipboard), finishing off with the top of the fastener on the inside of the book.

15. Drill a small hole through the reinforcements and the top and bottom book covers. (Be careful to place a protective mat under the book covers so that you don't cut into your book pages!) On the top flap, drill a centered hole 1″ in from the edge. On the bottom flap, drill a centered hole 3¼″ in from the edge.

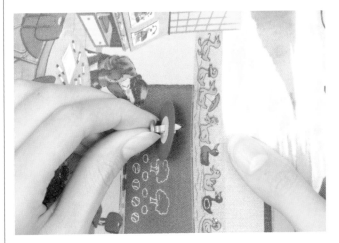

12. Punch 4 red ⅞″ circles and 4 yellow ⅜″ circles from the scraps of red and yellow cardstock.

13. Glue 2 red circles together and then glue yellow circles on the back and front of the red circles, centered as shown in the photo. Repeat for the second reinforcement. See page 20 for reinforcement instructions.

14. Close your book to plan the position of the reinforcements and thread.

16. Place a brad through the reinforcement and the cover on both the top and bottom flaps.

17. Tie red waxed linen thread underneath the reinforcement and tie a knot. Don't worry—no one will see the knot; it's just to keep the thread attached.

18. Fold the book covers up, and string tie the covers closed.

This folded cover is a nice, easy style that allows you to add any style of pages you want. I thought an accordion page would be a fun and fast gift for a coach, music teacher, or neighbor who may be moving. Just a little something to say how much you appreciate the special people in your life!

THANK YOU, COACH! BOOK

Finished size: 6½″ × 6½″

SUPPLIES

- Prepared fabric book cloth, cut to 6½″ × 12½″ (see pages 15–16 for instructions)

- Matching thread

- 1 sheet matching cardstock

- 1 sheet 19″ × 25½″ textured white art paper

- Glue

- Assorted baseball embellishments: EK Success

MAKING THE BOOK

1. With your sewing machine set to a decorative stitch, sew around the edges of the prepared fabric book cloth with matching thread (see page 17). Remember to start and stop where a fold will be so the stitching won't be obvious.

2. With the inside of the cloth cover facing you, fold the cover over 3¼″ from both sides. Gently crease these folds with a bone folder. You don't want the creases too sharp or the accordion won't fit into the cover.

3. Cut the art paper into 2 strips, 1 strip 6″ × 18¾″, 1 strip 6″ × 19¾″.

4. Using a stylus, a dry ballpoint pen, or your bone folder, score lines on the first piece of cut art paper (A) at 6¼″ and 12½″, measuring from the left. On the second piece of art paper (B), score lines at 6¼″, 12½″, and 18¾″, again measuring from the left (see illustration on page 61).

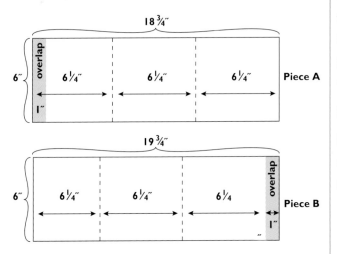

6. Cut a 6¼" x 6" piece of cardstock. This gives you a base to glue your accordion-folded art paper to. Using just a little glue, glue the cardstock to the back of the folded paper. Set aside to dry.

7. Once dry, center and glue the cardstock/art paper insert to the inside of the book cover.

8. Embellish the book as you like. I decorated both sides of the accordion so the team would be able to add pictures all around.

5. Glue Piece A to Piece B, overlapping the the 1˝ section of Piece A with the 1˝ section of Piece B. Once dry, fold it accordion style.

Well, here we are at the end of the book. After making it this far, you now know that you can mix any style of cover with just about any style of pages and closures. It's fun to mix and match to suit your own needs. Add embellishments, photos, fibers…just have fun creating your own books, whether they are skewer books or beyond!

Sources

Special thanks go to the following companies for supplying some of the products used in projects in this book.

7gypsies—Paper and embellishments
www.sevengypsies.com

All My Memories—Paper and embellishments
www.allmymemories.com

American Tag— Paper and embellishments
www.americantag.net

Autumn Leaves— Paper and embellishments
www.autumnleaves.com

Bazzill Basics— Paper and embellishments
www.bazzillbasics.com

Beacon Adhesives—Fabri-Tac
www.beaconcreates.com

Best Kept Secret—Fabrics
www.thebestkeptsecret.com

Big Horn Quilts—Fabrics
www.bighornquilts.com

Born to Quilt—Fabrics
www.borntoquilt.com

Blumenthal Lansing Company—La Mode buttons
www.buttonsplus.com

Canson—Art supply products
www.canson-us.com

Colorbök—Fabulous papers
www.colorbok.com

The Crafter's Pick—The Ultimate! glue
www.crafterspick.com

Creating Keepsakes Scrapbook Magazine—
Fonts, tips, and tricks
www.creatingkeepsakes.com

Creative Imaginations—Paper, embellishments, and more
www.cigift.com

Creative Impressions—Fleur d'Lis brads
www.creativeimpressions.com

Darice—Embellishments galore
www.darice.com

Die Cuts With a View—Die cutters
www.diecutswithaview.com

DMC—All types of threads
www.dmc.com

EK Success—Lots of embellishments, metal paper, and fibers
www.eksuccess.com

eQuilter—Fabrics
www.equilter.com

Fiskars—Scissors
www.fiskars.com

Flair Designs—Great dog and cat papers and embellishments
www.flairdesignsinc.com

FoofaLa—Distinctive products for crafters of all kinds
www.foofala.com

Glue-Dots International—Glue dots
www.gluedots.com

Hampton Art—Rubber stamps
www.hamptonart.com

Hancock's of Paducah—Fabrics
www.hancocks-paducah.com

Heidi Grace Designs—Paper and embellishments
www.heidigrace.com

Hirschberg Schutz & Co., Inc.—Embellishments, available at Michaels stores
www.michaels.com

Hoffman California Fabrics—Beautiful fabrics, including batiks
www.hoffmanfabrics.com

JHB International—Buttons
www.buttons.com

Jo-Ann Fabric & Crafts—General crafting shop
www.joann.com

Junkitz—Embellishments
www.junkitz.com

K&Company—Life's Journey line of scrapbooking supplies
www.kandcompany.com

Keepsake Quilting—Fabrics
www.keepsakequilting.com

Kelly Paper—Vellum-finish paper (lining paper for fabric cards)
www.kellypaper.com

KI Memories—Paper and embellishments
www.kimemories.com

Lasting Impressions—Paper and embellishments
www.lastingimpressions.com

Li'l Davis Designs—Paper and embellishments
www.lildavisdesigns.com

Limited Edition Rubber Stamps—Rubber stamps
www.limitededitionrs.com

Magic Scraps—Textured papers, file frames, and other fun embellishments in a variety of styles.
www.magicscraps.com

Making Memories—Rubber stamps, paper, and embellishments
www.makingmemories.com

Marcel Schurman—Embellishments
www.schurman.com

Marcella by Kay—Decorative papers and embellishments available at Target stores

Marvey—Ink pads and punches
www.uchida.com

Me & My Big Ideas—Fabric labels, sticker, papers, and more
www.meandmybigideas.com

Meri Meri—Accents
www.merimeri.com

Michael Miller Fabrics—Novelty, holiday, and sport fabrics
www.michaelmillerfabrics.com

Michael Miller Memories—Fabric paper
www.michaelmillermemories.com

Michaels stores—General crafting shop
www.michaels.com

My Mind's Eye—Papers and embellishments
www.mymindseyeinc.com

Offray—Ribbon and more ribbon
www.offray.com

Postmodern Designs Inc.—Rubber stamps
Email: postmoderndesign@aol.com

Provo Craft—Paper, embellishments, and more
www.provocraft.com

Ranger Crafts—Inks and stamp cleaners
www.rangerink.com

Rubber Baby Buggy Bumpers—Rubber stamps
www.rubberbaby.com

Sizzix—Personal die-cut machines and lots of fun dies to use in all your crafting projects.
www.sizzix.com

Stamper's Warehouse—General crafting shop
www.stamperswarehouse.com

Sticker Studio—Stickers, paper, and embellishments
www.stickerstudio.com

Therm O Web—HeatnBond Lite Iron-On Adhesive
www.thermoweb.com

Timeless Treasures—Wonderful novelty and gotta-have batik fabrics
www.ttfabrics.com

Tombow—Tape runners and more
www.tombowusa.com

Tsukineko—Inkpads and re-inkers
www.tsukineko.com

Westrim Crafts—Paper Bliss line of paper and embellishments
www.westrimcrafts.com

Wordsworth—Stamps, stickers, stencils, and more
www.wordsworthstamps.com

Xyron—Sticker, laminating, and "magneting" machine
www.xyron.com

About the Author

Sue Astroth was born in Southern California, where she lived until moving to Concord, California, in 1997. Sue has been a crafter her whole life—needle arts, quilting, and paper arts are her ongoing favorites. Most recently, she has been combining fabric and paper in unexpected ways.

In 2005 she appeared on the 2005 CHA Craft Special with Carol Duvall and on *Simply Quilts* with Alex Anderson, where she demonstrated her first book, *Fast, Fun & Easy Scrapbook Quilts*.

When she isn't in the studio creating new projects, she is either out collecting treasures for her cards and quilts, pruning her roses in the garden, or working at a local stamp, art, and scrapbook store where she gets lots of great ideas.

Sue doesn't look back…except to say thank you to her family and friends for the love and support she constantly receives from them along her artistic journey.

For more information, request a free catalog:

C&T Publishing, Inc.

P.O. Box 1456

Lafayette, CA 94549

(800) 284-1114

Email: ctinfo@ctpub.com

Website: www.ctpub.com

For quilting supplies:

The Cotton Patch—Mail Order

3405 Hall Lane, Dept. CTB

Lafayette, CA 94549

(800) 835-4418

Email: quiltusa@yahoo.com

Website: www.quiltusa.com

Note:

Fabrics and embellishments used in the projects shown may not be currently available.

 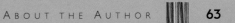

Great Titles from

C&T PUBLISHING